D1082761

Health and My Body

Rest Your Body

by Martha E. H. Rustad

PEBBLE
a capstone imprint

Pebble Explore is published by Pebble, an imprint of Capstone
1710 Roe Crest Drive
North Mankato, Minnesota 56003
www.capstonepub.com

**Library of Congress Cataloging-in-Publication Data is available on
the Library of Congress website.**
ISBN: 978-1-9771-2387-9 (library binding)
ISBN: 978-1-9771-2687-0 (paperback)
ISBN: 978-1-9771-2424-1 (eBook PDF)

Summary: Whether you like bedtime or not, sleep is important. But
why do we need to sleep? And what happens while we sleep? These
questions and more will be answered in this book.

Image Credits
Shutterstock: 3445128471, 27, Africa Studio, 18, Creativa Images,
6, digitalskillet, Cover, Iakov Filimonov, 25, jamesteohart, top 23,
Joshua Resnick, 24, JPC-PROD, 9, Lapina, 28, LeManna, bottom 23,
myboys.me, 15, pixfly, 5, photonova, design element throughout, PR
Image Factory, 13, Prostock-studio, 7, Rawpixel.com, 11, Rido, 8,
Romrodphoto, 17, VectorMine, 19, Yuganov Konstantin, spread 20-21,
26, Yuliya Evstratenko, 29

Editorial Credits
Editor: Christianne Jones; Designer: Sarah Bennett; Media Researcher:
Morgan Walters; Production Specialist: Laura Manthe

All internet sites appearing in back matter were available and
accurate when this book was sent to press.

Printed in the United States of America.
PA117

Table of Contents

Bold words are in the glossary.

Sleep and Rest

Everyone needs sleep. You spend about one-third of your life sleeping. Sleep gives your body and brain a chance to rest. Sleep keeps you well.

Babies and toddlers need the most sleep. They sleep 14 to 17 hours a day. Older kids need between 9 and 12 hours of sleep each night. Teens need eight to ten hours of sleep. Adults need 7 to 9 hours.

Sometimes you might feel tired during the day. This is a good time to rest. Resting is like a time-out for your body. At school, you might get a brain break or rest time.

There are lots of ways to rest your body. You can lie down and rest. You can sit, close your eyes, and take deep breaths. Just give your brain and body a break. Your body needs both rest and sleep to be your best.

Why Do We Need Sleep?

Our brains need sleep to work well. Even though you are resting, your brain keeps working. It helps us fall and stay asleep. It even helps us dream.

During sleep, our bodies are at work too. Sleep helps us get better when we are sick. Sleep can even help us grow!

When you feel sick, your body works to help you feel better. Sleep is one way your body helps you get well. When you sleep, your body is better able to fight what is making you sick. It makes tiny things called **proteins**. You need proteins to stay well.

Proteins are found in **cells**. Cells are the tiny building blocks that make up all plants and animals. These proteins help keep you healthy. If you don't get enough sleep, your body can't make these proteins.

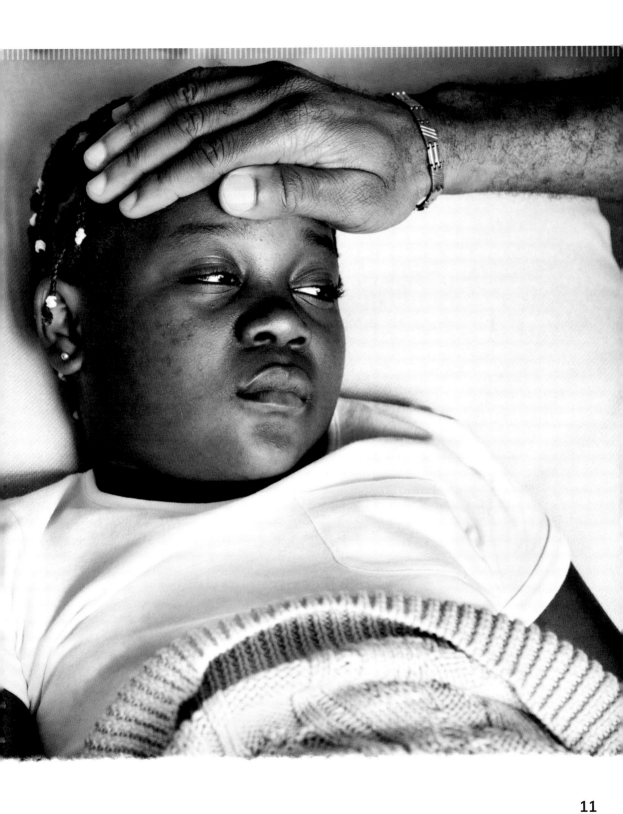

What If We Don't Sleep?

Think about the last time you didn't get enough sleep. How did you feel the next day?

You were tired. You might have been crabby. You might have felt sick.

A tired brain doesn't work very well. It might be hard to follow directions. You move more slowly. It's hard to do your best at school. That's why sleep is so important.

Your body can catch up from a few nights of bad sleep. But problems can start if you get too little sleep for a long time.

People who get too little sleep get sick more often. Their bodies are too run down to stay healthy.

Without sleep, the brain can't do its job. A tired brain has a hard time learning. It cannot remember new facts.

Stages of Sleep

It seems like nothing is happening when you are asleep. But so much is going on! Your body goes through many stages of sleep each night.

This first stage of sleep is the shortest. It is called **light sleep**. Your mind and body slow down. You start to drift off. You can still wake up easily.

The next stage is **intermediate sleep**. Your body continues to **relax**. Your eyes, brain, and muscles slow down more. Your heart rate slows down. You breathe more slowly. Even your body temperature goes down.

Then you go into deep sleep. It is also called **slow wave sleep**. It is very hard to wake up during this stage.

Stages of Sleep

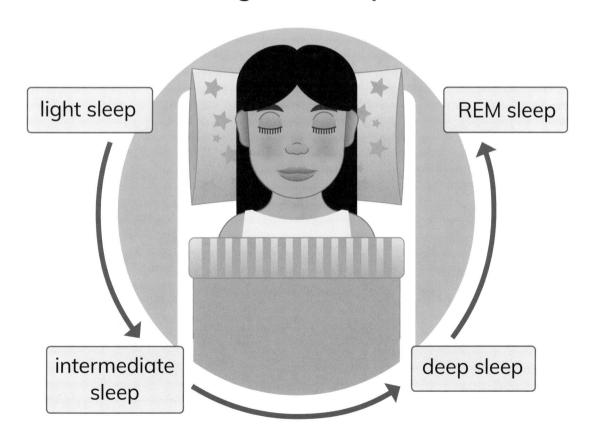

light sleep

REM sleep

intermediate sleep

deep sleep

During the last stage of sleep, you enter **REM**. This stands for rapid eye movement. Your eyes move back and forth behind closed eyelids.

During REM, your body is totally relaxed. But your brain is very busy. Your heart beats a little faster. Your breathing pattern changes.

You go through all the stages of sleep every night. In fact, you go through them four or five times.

Everyone has dreams.
Dreams happen during REM
sleep. But not everyone
remembers their dreams.
Why do people dream?
No one knows for sure.

Some people think dreams
are how the brain sorts what
you think and feel. Other
people think dreams come
from your brain going over
what happened during
the day. Still others think
dreams tell you what you
are worried about.

Getting Good Sleep

What you do during the day affects how you sleep at night. Follow a morning **routine**. Get up at the same time every day. Get dressed. Brush your teeth. Wash your face. Eat breakfast.

Be active every day. Your body needs to work hard. Then it will be ready to rest at night. Go outside! Take a walk. Go for a bike ride. Fresh air and sunshine make your body feel good.

Watch what you eat and drink. Too much sugar can make sleeping hard.

Turn off all electronics an hour before bed. They shine a blue light that wakes up your brain. Turn off the lights in your room. Keeping your room dark tells your brain it's time to slow down.

After a busy day, your body will be ready to sleep. Like you did in the morning, follow a routine.

Start getting your body ready for sleep an hour before bedtime. Put on pajamas. Brush your teeth. Wash your face. Go to bed at the same time every night.

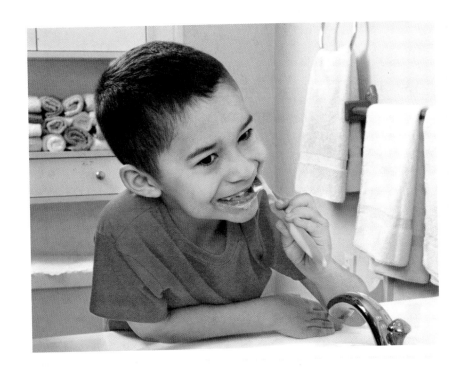

Sometimes it can be hard to fall asleep. Here are a few ideas if you don't feel tired.

- Take a warm bath.

- Read a book or listen to a story.

- Turn on a fan or **sound machine**.

- Put a heavy quilt or a weighted blanket on your bed.

Now close your eyes and go to sleep.

Sweet dreams!

Glossary

cell (SEL)—the tiny building block that makes up all plants and animals

intermediate sleep (in-tur-MEE-dee-it SLEEP)—the stage of sleep when your body fully relaxes

light sleep (LITE SLEEP)—first and shortest stage of sleep

protein (PROH-teen)—the thing found in all living plant and animal cells

relax (REE-laks)—to become less tight or stiff

REM (REM)—stands for rapid eye movement; happens during the deep sleep stage

routine (roo-TEEN)—a set of actions that become a habit

slow wave sleep (SLOH WAYV SLEEP)—the deepest stage of sleep

sound machine (SOUND muh-SHEEN)—a device that makes a steady, dull sound, such as ocean waves crashing or rain

Read More

Black, Vanessa. *Sleep*. Minneapolis: Jump!, 2017.

Gitlin, Marty. *Sleeping Better*. Hallandale, FL: Mitchell Lane, 2018.

Pipe, Jim. *You Wouldn't Want to Live without Sleep!* New York: Franklin Watts, 2016.

Internet Sites

Sleep for Kids
http://sleepforkids.org

Tips for Good Sleep
https://www.cdc.gov/chronicdisease/resources/infographic/children-sleep.htm

What Sleep Is and Why All Kids Need It
https://kidshealth.org/en/kids/not-tired.html

Index